MW01532037

Well Behaved Cowgirls

A Musical Memoir

by

Lois Berg

Well Behaved Cowgirls:
A Musical Memoir

Production and Distribution through
Only Wonder Media LLC

Thanksgivings

Gratitude is an action.
A few folks who are in my life of constant movement:

- ✓ Nadia Bruce-Rawlings – editor, spiritual guide, uplifting soul-sister.
- ✓ Jay Voorhees – chief layout dream manager.
- ✓ Cecilia Diana & Jenessa – my daughters and cheerleading squad.
- ✓ Matraca – my older sister, mentor and first power source.
- ✓ Ron Berg – my amazing confidant and living father of nuclear physics.
- ✓ Eric Berg – my baby brother and sweet graphic artist of my trade mark.
- ✓ Michael St. Leon – my musical engineer who has been working for me for next to nothing for over twenty years because he believes in my music.
- ✓ Linda Phifer – my cousin who is responsible for all photos.
- ✓ Aunt Sudie – our music row matriarch who brought us to Nashville in the first place.
- ✓ Liz Reese – who continues to save women's lives in Lebanon, Tennessee.
- ✓ Dan Keen – my professor from Belmont who gave me this idea along with David Maddox. (I hear smart people)
- ✓ Charles Lackey – my banjo beast.
- ✓ And the oldest dude I continue to rely upon who has no last name – GOD.

Table of Contents

Introduction
Knowing Lois

I think I probably heard Lois before I ever saw her.

I had stopped by a local coffee house in the village where we both live, and I heard a woman's plaintive cry coming from inside. When I glanced in, there was a woman with a guitar singing her heart out. The southern roots were unmistakable, and she sang with authority: a kind of Janis Joplin on steroids. The songs were about pain, and heartbreak, and longing, and the old man standing beside her playing the guitar looked like he had lived out those stories in spades. I'd come to find out later that they both had.

"Who's that?" I asked the barista.

"That's Lois," he said, as if it should be obvious who she was and as if it was my fault that I had never heard of her.

That feeling of confusion in what seemed like a simple question never really went away.

That was five years ago know, and a lot of water has passed under the bridge in my friendship with Lois. We finally met in a church basement drinking bad coffee after a group of alcoholics had shared their stuff. I was the "adopted pastor dude" who preached upstairs and had come downstairs to see what this recovery thing was all about. Lois was there as a woman in recovery, and she didn't hesitate to share about what the program had done for her, how God had her back, and how grateful she was for being free of the demons that had haunted her for many years.

What I would learn over time was that this short, loud, and talented woman was a force of nature, who had lived a hard life but who had found the power to be transformed into something new. She was open and honest in ways beyond the average person in society, and that openness and honesty would spring forth in the songs she wrote. When Lois puts her mind to doing something . . . well it's probably best to get out of the way because it's bound to happen. This was a woman who could move from the shelter to the college campus with ease, and who knew that she had been blessed beyond belief. This book is an expression of that belief that God has big things in store for her, and if people don't believe it then that's their problem, not hers.

Earlier today she called. "I'm so excited about this book," she said. She went on to tell me about an upcoming tour, the CD she was putting together as a companion to this book, and all the things she has going in her life. But even so she understands that she continues to be a work in progress – a person living one day at a time. Once upon a time in her life she was a *Crazy Angel* (as she writes in song) but today she is also a *Well Behaved Cowgirl* just waiting to see what the one who healed her has in store for her.

During the past five years I've been Lois's boss, her confidant, her employer, and her friend. It's because of Lois that I had my first ever (and probably my last) honky-tonk performance on Lower Broadway in Nashville. Lois pushes me to do things that I probably wouldn't do on my own (such as publishing this book!) because she has no fear and invites all who will come to join her on this crazy ride we call life.

So hold on to your hats as you saddle up and hear Lois talk about her life. There's a lot to be learned in that story, and watch out because you might find yourself up on a stage next to a rebel yelling tornado who knows more than anyone I know that life is meant to be lived.

Rev. Jay Voorhees

Angel in Disguise

She sees blue diamonds when she cries. She sees beauty in every eye.
Sometimes dark and cold like ice promising paradise

Sometimes blue sometimes green beautiful like the sea Sometimes love but mostly greed

Chorus:
But they're just angels along the way waiting patiently for their wings
They're just angels along the way angels along the way angels along the wayeeeeeah

She feels closer to grace with lines across her face And there's no mirror that can change her mind She knows that she's an angel in disguise

Chorus:
She's an angel along the way waiting patiently for her wings
She's an angel along the road and when you meet her you probably will not know
She's an angel, she's an angel, she's an angel, she's angel.

I was living in a large Victorian turn-of-the-century home filled with eight other women. We all had chores to do every day to keep the home running efficiently. My husband had filed for divorce and was waiting for my response; I wasn't quite sure how to respond. It was very confusing, so I asked my spiritual guide. Her response was, as usual, the same: pray and ask God to reveal the answer to your question. All of the women in my house had said that my husband's only intention was to take everything from me, including my children. In retrospect, they were absolutely correct in their assumptions.

It was a spring day in Nashville. Everything was blooming, and each day was another miracle for me: waking up instead of coming to. I still do get on my knees in the morning and at night and pray with my hands together for the spirit of the universe to reveal his or her powerful forces to me. That day at Krystal, a gigantic mountain of an Indian healer walked into my restaurant with another sober friend of mine for lunch. His name is Lou Medicine Bird White Eagle. Lou could tell that I had a question for him because he has this gift. Lou said, "What is it that you are seeking?" I was totally honest with him, and I said, "My true love." "Hmmm this is good," Lou responded. "I have something for you today." Lou gave me a pink rock. He placed this firmly into my hands, and he said, "take this to the water which I feel is close to your home, bring with you a candle for the light before the break of dawn, and your white sage to burn for your ceremony."

I was puzzled. "Ceremony?" I asked. Lou explained that his job was as an Indian healer, and that he did this throughout the world for different tribes of people all of the time. Lou said that my answer may not be exactly what I was seeking, but the spirit of the Universe will answer my question in time if I truly ask and perform my ceremony.

So I went home with my pink rock that weekend to my tiny little cottage in Lebanon to take care of my home and my children. There was a beautiful little creek that flowed through our driveway, which had caught my eye originally when I found my home online. Lou had said that because my need was deeper than this, that I should take my question to deeper waters. So I went out into the deeper waters across the street from my home. It was weird, and precarious, but not unusual for me to be there because we had gone fishing together as a family prior to my husband's need for divorce. I traversed the rocky trail and stood, as Lou had suggested, with my lit candle for light. I burned my white sage, and I held my pink rock out to each corner of the universe: North, South, East and West. I asked, "Please, powers of the universe, reveal to me exactly my true love." I dropped the pink rock and went about my day.

It took two years.

I ran into Lou Medicine Man White Eagle in March 2011. I was sooo excited to see this mountain of a man again, to give him my good news. I hugged him with full force. He remembered me, and he said, "So? What did the universe reveal to you?" I said "Lou!!! It was something that was inside of me all along!!" Lou said calmly, "Hmmm, of course this is good." I said, "It was my music! My true love was and always has been writing, and singing, and creating music!"

My true love was revealed, and today I will never lose it even when my spirit has passed on into the energy of the universe. My children and my grandchildren will know what my mother never knew, what I now know. My hope for you is that if you are having a struggle with your question, that you find your truth, salvation and gifts from the inside as well.

Lois

Chapter 1
Crazy Angel

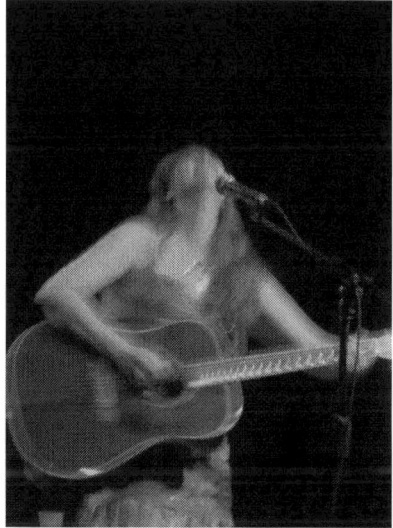

Sin on her mind, love in her eyes.
Dancing through clouds
with a 3 step glide
Big belt buckle, tight blue jeans.
Cutest little angel any cowboy has seen
She got cowgirl boots,
butterflies on the side.
They're so cool; man,
I wish they were mine
She can mix and mingle
like her wings are on fire
I can see cherubs
talking about their desire,
how they love to watch her
From every angle,
but no one wants to mess around
with no crazy angel

Mama's just a crazy angel now,
raising hell in Heaven
dancing through clouds
Mama's just a crazy angel now, but I know I'm going to see her someday,
somehow

There's usually not cussing at Heaven's gate
She wasn't just fussing, she'd rather been late
She was kicking and screaming profanities
I'm surprised she made it wouldn't get down on her knees
But Saint Peter just waved her right on in
When he noticed Jesus' big goofy grin

Mama's just a crazy angel now, raising hell in heaven dancing through clouds
Mama's just a crazy angel now, but I know I'm going to see her someday somehow

The pilgrimage back to Harlan County, Kentucky takes about 4 hours from my home in Nashville, Tennessee. It is still about the same as I remembered it from 40 years ago. Nothing has changed much there. There's still just one stop light in the tiny little town of Wallins Creek where my Mama grew up. The soda pop store is still standing, though grown over with ivy and memories. The growth of the vines has all but enveloped the little white clapboard building where we would get our Coca Colas and M80 firecrackers -- our small arsenal of weapons and sugar for energy. Old family trailers still have satellite dishes larger than the home. My Meemaw, is alive and well at 97 years old. Icie is my grandma, or Meemaw as we call her. She's a willowy lady and sharp, as folks say, for her age. The coal mining town is tucked in between two mountains, and it is difficult for people to find it.

Coal mines are pitch black, cold with possibilities of energy and fuel. Manmade caves dug into the sides of mountains in Kentucky, like mole-holes. Digging for coal, looking for energy. My family history on my mother's side begins in the darkness and echoes of caves there. Where the life of our family began to struggle and to celebrate to the extreme in the holler of Wallins Creek.

Meemaw holds me tight, closer with more strength than she should have at her age. Tough English/Cherokee Indian heritage. Meemaw's house is always filled with freshly cooked homemade biscuits, and beans, and cornbread. Pinto beans made up the majority of my mother's bone marrow structure. I know that is why I continue to cook them up whenever I need a taste of home.

Somehow they went through the Depression, and everyone survived through to adulthood. Four girls and two boys. Mama was the second-to-the-youngest of the bunch but the youngest girl.

There's a bunkhouse at the end of the road sits next to the main house; Meemaw calls it the "sin" house. The bunk house has a great big front porch on the front of it. That's where I sang during one of our wing-dings and got super hooked into music. We lined the bunk house porch with amplifiers, and Papaw picked the banjo, and my Aunts would sing and play till the wee, wee hours of the morning. Wallins Creek is still considered a "dry" county. That never stopped any of the drinking and carousing though. Papaw had two affairs: one with Meemaw, and the other with moonshine; and they were always in conflict.

Papaw made a living in the coal mines. The darkness is hard to describe; it has its own energy. Took a few lives every once in a while. I guess that could be why the struggles and celebrations were both so extreme. I guess they were considered hillbilly because they lived on the side or the bottom of the mountains. Digging for coal for a living, making moonshine, music, and children.

The air is cleaner, brisker, and family life is simple there. The garden still brings in the majority of the veggies. They still kill hogs for meat down the road. Fishing and hunting bring in plenty of food.

Every time I go back home with my Meemaw, I feel like I belong there and had just been a seed caught on the wind for too long. There isn't anything like it. The Cumberland Gap smells like musky pine trees that want to grab me and keep me prisoner there.

Though living in Nashville is the only thing that I am used to, my bones somehow know why I feel at home in Wallins Creek. My sister says that because of our Cherokee heritage, we have intuition that normal folks don't have. Sometimes I believe her; sometimes I don't.

My mother was a hillbilly terrorist. Mama created her own ride by rolling up like a roly poly into the middle of a tire, then launching off the side of the mountain to roll down into the holler. Dizzy and exhilarated, no thought about danger. She was talking, reading, and singing extraordinarily beyond expectations at a very early age. Little Icie was academically quicker than all of the other children. She was a dazzling, mysterious diamond in the rough in a coal mining town. Teachers were quite aware of her gifts. Monk (her nickname) was singled out amongst her peers. The children misunderstood her enigmatic chaos. Her educators gave Meemaw an opportunity to bring my mother to another school where she would be challenged. Meemaw just said "nah, I reckon she's fine right here."

Being different in elementary school in a tiny coal mining town would be tough for most folks, but it wasn't for my Mama. She was just such a charismatic, entertaining, little spirit that folks were immediately drawn to her personality. School was a whiz for Mama: naturally talented with singing and always whirling around into new ideas.

It was always magical, the voices of my Aunts and Mama blending together as they sang perfect harmonies. They were like hillbilly gypsies, pining for new life through music. My Aunts formed their own band, and Meemaw was their manager, by the time they were all large enough to hold instruments. Meemaw made her girls home-made matching dresses to wear to their live shows on Renfro Valley radio. I guess I was destined to follow in their footsteps all along as a singer-songwriter today. Just part of my bone marrow structure, like beans and cornbread.

My mother's curiosity got her pregnant. My big sister was conceived in the back seat of a 1963 silver Chevy Bel Air on her prom night. The man was married at the time, and that changed the trajectory of her life forever. It was a real blow to Papaw. Papaw just 'bout beat Mama to death to find out the father's name, and that was the main reason Mama fled town. If Papaw had found out, our family's honor would have been taken back with one shot from his rifle for sure. Murder was quite common for that kind of problem in Wallins Creek. Folks wouldn't blink an eye over sudden death for resentments. It hasn't changed much there either. Thankfully my Mama's older sister, Sudie Mae, had already left town to follow her musical dreams to Nashville.

Undirected brilliance appears to be chaos to normal folks. My Mama was super-star gorgeous. Funny, witty, gifted, and scathingly mean when she started drinking. As kids, we had to walk around the house alert to the possibility that Mama was tying one on. I still have a huge scar on the back of my

15

head where I was beaten with the buckle of the belt. Lots of blood comes from a head wound. My sister said all the blood and screaming were horrific. I only have a scar from it; my mind apparently blocked out everything that occurred that evening.

Mama married a few times. Once to my father, Ron Berg, a brilliant nuclear physicist who luckily adopted my sister, and then to Dave Kirby. In between the marriages, my mother also hooked into a rage-aholic. He beat us kids, and was always negative towards my mother's aspirations as a songwriter. As children we would listen to his barrage of verbal degradations towards Mama. Not sure what my mother saw in the guy except he was cute on the outside; certainly nothing cute on the inside.

Mama kicked me out of her home when I was just 11 years old, during one of her many drunken rages. I had stood up to the sexual predator / boyfriend and threatened to call the police on him before he disappeared out of our lives forever. Mama and I had gotten drunk together, and she had tried her best to convince me that I owed him an apology. I knew right from wrong even back then and said, "No way!"

My mother moved on after that relationship to marry her second husband, Dave Kirby. Now y'all talk about drinking buddies! Dave was writing with Merle Haggard at that time while married to Leona Williams. They were drinking, songwriting, singing, running dawgs.

I never felt safe in any home again until 2009. That's from 1978 until 2009. I made the same decisions as my mother did: abusive alcoholic relationships. Same cycle, same result.

My crazy, beautiful, talented, smart, witty, delirious, angel; my Mama died just a few weeks after she turned 40 years old.

She's just a crazy angel up in Heaven now. I know that she's raising hell up there. And, she is the reason why I am having success with my music here on earth. Shortly after my mother took her last breaths on earth Aunt Sudie said, "I sure hope you find some happiness in Heaven, little sister, 'cause you just never seemed to find it here."

Sisters know more about each other than anybody else, that's my experience.

Today I am the mother of two girls; both of them are singing and writing music. I am working on having my children pass down the musical gifts that my Mama passed along to me. Mama taught me my first "C" chord when I was just ten years old. We were always singing at the dinner table and still do. My oldest daughter is now twenty years old, and she's been in the studio with me since she could walk. The Switchyard Studio is underneath a big log cabin and even smells like the bunkhouse where I began singing for the first time in Harlan County, Wallins Creek, Kentucky, so many years ago.

I wrote the song *Crazy Angel* for my Mama. It also brought me to the Williamsburg Live Songwriting Competition in New York City.

When I got back home into Nashville after my horrific divorce from the second abusive relationship, there was just one song in my BMI catalogue: named *Crazy Angel* it amazingly still had my maiden name on it! It was a sign from God that Mama was still with me.

Chapter 2
Sudie Mae

Born under a blue moon in Harlan Kentucky
Hair as black as coal from the mines
Moved her wild roots to 16th avenue
Way back in 1969

All of you wayward worn out musicians
She bring in year after year from the cold
Fix up your broken dreams with duct tape
and a butter knife
How she lift you up then she save your soul

SUDIE CALLAWAY

Sudie Mae...Sudie Mae...
music row matriarch...
she'll have a hit song one day.

All of you wayward worn out musicians
She bring in year after year from the cold
Fix up your broken dreams with duct tape and a butter knife
How she lift you up then she save your soul

Sudie Mae...
Sudie Mae....
 music row matriarch ....
she'll have a hit song one day.

The safest place that I can remember from my childhood was that sacred place encircled within the arms of my Aunt Sudie. My Aunt Sudie would wrap me up into her big bosom, and I felt warm and snuggled there. When we needed something to eat at Aunt Sudie's house, we could raid her pantry. We always did, because we were starved as children living on hand-me-down bologna sandwiches. At Aunt Sudie's house, there was music, magic, and laughter all the time. I always knew just how much she loved me. She still says to me today that she loves me like I am her own child.

Sudie, my mother's oldest sister, is magical. She is the reason why my family ended up here in Nashville. Aunt Sudie was bitten by the music bug from a very early age. When other elementary school children were carrying their books and shot guns to school, Aunt Sudie carried her guitar. Children in those days would go hunting on the way home and carry their squirrels or rabbits they had plugged home to cook. My Aunt Sudie carried her guitar everywhere she went, and she received ridicule for her ambitions. She was not swayed by the peer pressures of Harlan County elementary mentality, though.

Sudie Mae began teaching herself how to play guitar by ear and was soon able to sing along in her sweet voice. She was quite adept at picking her own bass line while playing her songs at the same time. The holler in Kentucky was filled with her music, and Icie, her mother, encouraged her daughter to continue her pursuits. Icie became the cheerleader of sorts for her daughter, and Aunt Sudie was the leader of the band. Sudie got her sisters involved, and they became the Calloway Sisters. Aunt Clara played a stand-up bass that was as big as she was. My Mama sang harmonies when she got big enough, and Aunt Coleida played banjo, and together that family blend of harmonies was perfectly mixed. Icie Calloway, known as Meemaw, made her girls matching dresses and pumped them up with her own belief that they would be super-stars shooting. Aunt Sudie marched herself down to the local radio show called Renfro Valley, known as Kentucky's Country Music Capital!

When I was just a little bitty thing, running wild in the holler during our trips back home to Harlan, we had huge wing-dings on the bunkhouse porch. Meemaw called it the "sin" house. Harlan is still a dry county, and there's nowhere to get booze close by, but my family always had that available. Grandpa made his own white lightning concoctions called "moonshine." Moonshine must have gotten its name because it had to be made in the moonlight up on the mountain and out of sight from the law.

We had huge bonfires and music, and we had the bunk house porch lined with amplifiers for the wing-dings in the holler. The music rang on into the evening and well into the wee morning hours. My first time in front of a microphone was on that big bunk house porch, singing harmony with my Aunt Clara to the song *You Are My Sunshine*.

There was some small ounce of power there with my voice being amplified into the evening smells of home. The bonfire jumping and keeping time with the laughter and whoops and hollers echoing into my childhood memories. I left my doubts about my life-path on that wooden porch that night. I knew that I would be some sort of entertainer for the rest of my days. The music bug may have crept up into my mind and nested during the darker days of my life, but it has always resurfaced ever stronger than before.

Sudie Mae left her home to successfully become one of the band members in Mel Tillis' band, before Mel became a big star. I have been told that when I was an angry little thing and was asked by "Uncle Mel" for some "sugar," I ran down the hallway and punched him square in the eye. Mel flipped backwards and plopped down on the floor holding his eye and exclaimed "...D...D...D...D...oris ain't gonna believe th...th...this!" I had given Uncle Mel a "black eye." Aunt Sudie has many stories about how I was a tiny terrorist with an angel's face.

I was so proud to be sweet little feisty Lois in my Aunt Sudie's eyes. I ran to her arms when the world became too angry for me to heal. Even now, in my Aunt Sudie's safe world, I am just a singer/songwriter that has everything working for me to blaze a trail into legendary paths. My Aunt Sudie lets me dream big. I am in awe of how many people that have said the exact same thing about my Aunt Sudie. She's the most amazing lady of faith and so super talented with her voice, her playing, her writing. Everything about my Aunt Sudie is sticky and sweet, just like honey. In fact, it was my Aunt Sudie that also told me exactly how sweet I was, and that my former husband was a loser. I love, love, love my sweet Aunt Sudie and want my children to have a special place in her heart, because there we cannot be harmed.

It was my Aunt Sudie who took me and my first child into her home when I found the crack cocaine in the basement of my first daughter's father. It was my Aunt Sudie who I called first, because I knew she would be able to help me and my daughter escape the drug-house I was living in. I guess you could say that I was rather naïve about drug addicts as well as alcoholics.

The first time I ran to my Aunt Sudie's safe haven was when I was 29 years old and my first baby was a one-year-old. I showed up at her doorstep with my baby in tow, disheveled, scared, angry at myself, and confused about what to do next. Me and Aunt Sudie prayed to God to find me and my baby girl a home that would be safe. God answers prayers of the righteous: that prayer was answered in one week. God supplied a tiny basement apartment in a brick home, basically in the back yard of my cousin's house. Aunt Sudie's prayers are powerful reminders today. I couldn't have asked for a safer place close to family.

My favorite song on my first album is of my Aunt Sudie singing all of the harmonies on *Home* for me with her granddaughter playing guitar.

Aunt Sudie also introduced me to Jesus. She has this great big room my Uncle Jim built out of the stones and granite. Uncle Jim also got himself a few hernias along with this grand room. We call it The Compound because they continued adding even another mother-in-law home onto the back of it. There was a pool table in the rec room with a gigantic fireplace. There was a big comfy golden bowl-shaped chair;

everyone called it the bird's nest. That's where I got my first taste of salvation. I was curious about church at that time, because a little girl next door to me had brought me to Sunday school. Aunt Sudie was the only other person that I was aware of besides Meemaw that ever talked about spirituality. She put her arms around me in that big bird's nest and hugged me like I meant something to her and asked me if I believed in Jesus Christ, and I said, "Yes I guess I do." I still recall how warm that circle of love felt, and I now have more faith because of Sudie Mae Calloway saving my soul. She never really went to church, but she was an avid Sunday morning TV-church worshipper.

Aunt Sudie Mae wrapped my dreams up my whole life, even in the midst of my chaotic, failed relationships and hardships. She wraps me up in love and salvation and duct tapes my dreams back together, feeds me chicken soup, and I carry on.

Chapter 3

Well Behaved Cowgirls

She was just 16 when she knew she had to go
Don't need a GED to join the rodeo
So she headed down the road wearing high top tennis shoes
Kicking up dust and memories and dreams she plans to choose

Because well behaved cowgirls, don't know how to rope, rarely
Learn how to ride. Because well behaved cowgirls rarely play the game
With loaded dice.

So she headed down the road wearing high top tennis shoes
Kicking up dust and memories and dreams she plans to choose
And her Mama knew to change her babies mind would be no use
Cause she had that stubborn determination inside of her too

Because well behaved cowgirls don't know how to rope, rarely
Learn how to ride. Because well behaved cowgirls rarely play the game
With loaded dice.

Harlan County, Kentucky is tucked in between mountains and coal mines and is a difficult place to find if you've never been there. The folks there are tough. They have been isolated by floods, coal mining, drug and alcohol addiction, as well as educational struggles that extend into the next generation. Mama was touted as such a nimble climber that she was described as a "monkey." That description followed her into her adult life, and her closest friends referred to her lovingly as Monk. Monk was born in Harlan County, and she always went to the extreme edge of her curiosity. Monk was more than just a dreamer; she was a doer. She was a climber of mountains, trees, rocks, railroad bridges, and boys. My mother was adept at anything that she set her mind to.

Monk was the youngest girl in that bunch of five siblings, so by the time my mother came into the world, Meemaw was tired. Today, my Meemaw is still kicking at ninety-seven years old and is an artist, a painter of oil on canvas, of still lives.

Monk's teenage pregnancy was the reason that she left to live in Oak Ridge, Tennessee. It was a dark time for her, because she left my sister at an orphanage for two days as a newborn. My sister almost wasn't in my life. Monk had every intention of giving her baby up for adoption. Grandpa just about beat Mama to death to find out the name of the father to eliminate him. Mama fled to live with her Aunt in Oak Ridge. My sister's father was a lesbian named Marie. That's on her birth certificate. Mama had my sister and gave her up for adoption before Aunt Sudie stepped in. Aunt Sudie begged the nurses to see her niece, and they let her. Thankfully Mama couldn't do it. She went back to the orphanage to retrieve my sister, just in the nick of time. She carried on with her life, forever changed by such a huge responsibility at such a young age.

Monk was a baby raising a baby. She went on living with her Aunt in Oak Ridge, Tennessee. She got a job working at a dime store. My sister got really fat from all the attention and food. My sister looked like a huge tub of love in those black and white photos of her first days on the earth. Monk looked like a beautifully happy child alongside her daughter. It wasn't the perfect picture, but my Mama made it work.

I wonder if my sister has ever felt abandoned because of the tumultuous entry she had to go through those few weeks of her beginnings here on earth. I believe we begin to hear and feel everything that happens from inside of the womb. I guess that is why some cultures protect their women from any upheavals while they are pregnant and even up to six weeks after. My mom, however, was far from protected.

My father stepped into the picture one hot summer day in Oak Ridge, Tennessee. His future bride, my mom, just happened to be working at the drug store where he stopped for directions. Love: it's an electrical energy that radiates from the inside and leaps up into our hearts. It creates a pumping, thumpin', animalistic energy that brings us close to each other. There's an immediate friction from the surge of heat that happens naturally, and then our bodies behave with instinctual drive. Love seems to attack at the exact moment we have that heightened sense of awareness. It takes a moment before feelings can catch up to words. I believe that we feel love long before we can express it. This is how I view my mother and father's first intimate exchange. It is mostly from a few bits and pieces of what I have heard through the years. Even though it ended in divorce, it will always be the only original love story that I was a part of.

My father, born on the same day as Albert Einstein, looked like a very young Kevin Costner. He was Vanderbilt nuclear physics student who studied at the Oak Ridge Nuclear Reactor. His parents owned a dairy farm in Luck, Wisconsin, therefore this brilliant student could be traced back to a farm and further back to Scandinavian blood. My father was, and still is, a very intelligent, open-minded fellow, though a bit lacking in regard to street smarts. Daddy was simply asking for directions to where the swimming pool was that day. I seriously doubt that he knew he would soon be married and have an instant family. Monk gave directions and promptly went home to get her swim suit. Monk, in her predatory mode, went to the swimming pool and found my father just coming out of the water, so she stepped on his head. It was love at first fight.

Monk said that when Daddy came by for their first date, he didn't even blink when he saw my sister. He took my sister into his arms and never ever looked back. In fact, my father adopted my sister, and she still has our same last name. They married, and they moved back to Nashville for Daddy to continue his education at Vanderbilt. I arrived in 1967, and we all lived on Vanderbilt Place above my Aunt Sudie and Uncle Jim.

The marriage didn't last long after the birth of my little brother...Mama shredded my father's heart. Monk found another man named Dave Kirby to marry, who at that time was writing with Merle Haggard. They were always busy partying together, and when my sister was just sixteen, she slipped away from the house. She was *not* a well-behaved cowgirl, ever! The home she ran to was where Brian Rawlings lived while he was going to school at Belmont. Brian knew that harboring a sixteen-year-old "jail bait" was asking for trouble. Brian brought my sister to a friend, Bobby Braddock's home. That evening Bobby and my sister co-wrote her first hit-song together. That song was called *Faking Love*, released by T.G. Sheppard and Karen Brooks.

Chapter 4
Forever Together

Adam and Eve never needed therapy, rumor has it they got along
The only temptation it grew on a tree and then paradise was gone

Chorus
They weren't fighting and angry and calling it quits when the thunder from the
devil started rolling in and maybe it's the struggle that kept them strong
And forever together was never too long

Johnny and June they sang their own tune through the darkenss in the spotlight.
The man in black said she hung the moon now their on a golden
Stage in the sky

Chorus
They ain't fighting and angry and calling it quits when the thunder from
The devil started rolling in, and maybe it's the struggle that kept them strong
And forever together was never too long

Bridge
It's all about what you see after love at first sight. Sometimes you just got to learn
how to love someone you don't ....like

We ain't fighting and angry and calling it quits when the thunder from the devil
starts rolling in and maybe it's the struggle that keeps us strong and forever
together is never too long

And forever together is never too long

35

If it's difficult, maybe God has a better plan.

My songs portray my outlook on life in a whimsical, magical kind of way: they are therapy for me. Kindness includes the truth. I wish I had my own perfect marriage to someone. It hasn't happened yet. I guess a portion of those poor choices came from what I learned from my childhood. The stars seem to reflect this.

Perhaps we weren't even meant to be together forever as humans. I don't know. I do know that I inherited a few of my mother's traits: opinionated, determined, feisty ball of fire and energy that she was. Hell on high heels. I also have a few of my father's traits: intelligent, observant, studious, problem-solver. I'm the very best of both of them.

I look at the black and white photographs of my mother and father's wedding day, and it appears as if they were quite happy. There is one in particular that I have, still hanging on the wall in my living room, when they were eating their wedding cake. My mother has that wild look in her eyes, and she is holding a piece of wedding cake in her bare hands. She's got one finger in her mouth, and my father is standing behind her in his white tuxedo observing with joyful amusement. He still has a rather detached way of viewing the world and people around him. He is a nuclear physicist in constant observation of life: the ultimate scientific experiment.

My mother, on the other hand, was just the exact opposite. Diving into things headfirst and making a huge mess. Brilliant chaos and methodical detachment. I view their pairing as oil and water.

My Aunt Sudie reminded me of how explosive the pairing was. My mother's anger came fierce and unexpected; my father's response to things flying towards him included calmness somehow! My mother being the tornado; my father the eye of the storm. The marriage didn't last long, but it did last long enough to bring me and my brother into the world.

I remember dishes breaking behind my father's head, and my father's response being "Yes dear." I still relate with my father today and communicate efficiently with him. I never could carry on a conversation with my mother. I don't know why, because people still say that I act just like her. Perhaps this is the main reason why we couldn't communicate, because we were exactly alike. I will never know.

I do know that my father never laid an angry hand on my mother during her explosive outbursts. Hurt people hurt other people…my mother was from a long line of wild roots from Kentucky, and that unresolved anger always seemed to show up at the strangest times.

I also know that my father was always buried in books and studying. One day I dipped my feet into a bucket of blue paint, while Mama was gone, and Daddy had disappeared into his books. The paint felt so smooth and squishy on my feet, I couldn't resist it. I walked around on our hard wood floors, leaving tiny five-year-old paisley blue foot prints throughout the house. It was awesomely exhilarating.

My sister was lucky that he brought her around with him to school. In fact, during this time, my sister wrote her first song on some computer paper, and my father was so proud of his little adopted daughter. He brought the writing to my mother to present it to her as a gift. The song was called *Rock Around Town*. My sister went on to become a legendary songwriter and is now known as Nashville's poet. Our lives continue to run parallel to each other today, though I have yet to receive the national recognition that my big sister has.

To say that my mother was unsettled would be an understatement. I still have no clue why my mother ran off. Who would divorce a doctor who loved you!? She never found happiness. But whenever she sat down with her guitar, there were moments of peace.

I do know that because of the amount of times that she moved us as kids after the divorce, that she could have started her own company called "3 kids and a Truck." We moved to eleven different schools within Tennessee from kindergarten on up to 5th grade. Looking back, I never had any best friends and was always the new kid trying to find my own niche. I had to make friends quickly, because I knew that we would be gone again soon. If the Department of Children's Services had gotten wind of the inconsistency, we probably would have been removed from the home today.

I remember our life after the divorce as my mother became more obsessed with alcohol and her main drug: abusive relationships. It always started with the alcohol though. I know now that she was most likely an alcoholic.

My mother wanted to be a singer/songwriter. I found some poems that my mother wrote, in a box full of memories that my Aunt Sudie gave to me. Mama had a way of writing rather stream of conscience with a few hints of her inner most feelings wrapped around the prose. It does appear, at least at this time, that she was still in love with my father. The date is 1972, and they lived on Blair Boulevard in Nashville. I was five years old then.

ICIE BERG (MONK) 1972

The morning comes
When you open your eyes

Day begins
When you kiss me

My heart starts beating
When your hand moves across the bed/in search of me

Night moves in

When you close your eyes
The day
The sun
The world has died

I'm jealous of the night
Sometimes I hate the darkness
It steals you from me
And makes you move away
Sleep untangles your arms - our legs
From the vine we were

41

Night is my enemy
When it takes you from me

Chapter 5

Play Me

Play me like the bow
on the strings of a cello
Play me like the boat
on the sea of mellow

Chorus:
Play me play me
play me like a cello

Bridge:
I'm a soul fire
a Maserati going
one hundred miles an hour
I'm a raging wild fire
only you can quench my desire
If only you

Chorus:
Play me play me
play meeeeeee like a cello

I had survived the very bottom of Mama's demoralization with her. My sister and brother had fled to Daddy's a year before. The home in Madison, Tennessee was overrun with cockroaches. Me and my little brother, before he left, would crunch cockroaches for fun as they ran underneath the carpeting. We didn't have heat, so we used the stove and some stand up heaters. Food and safety were scarce. My mother's total downfall was imminent. We still refer to that large stone house in Madison, Tennessee as "Alcatraz." It had six apartments inside of it. My mother found me smoking one of her cigarettes, and in a rage, she physically threw me down the back steps. I was eleven, and I wasn't in a safe house. I knew that it was the alcohol that was slowly destroying my mother. I hated it.

Daddy came in the middle of the night to retrieve me from the hell hole. I remember having a trash bag full of clothes and my teddy bear. I fell asleep in the back of my daddy's car and woke up with crunchy snot and cold tears and a new life in Indiana. My father lived in an apartment complex and was working at Methodist Hospital in Indianapolis. I started school and began to rediscover my talents. One of my talents was to blend into the crowd and that included my father's cult. The Way Ministry was a cult that met in homes and people spoke in tongues. I wanted to be accepted by my father so badly that I jumped right in. I was speaking in tongues and studying the bible. The bible studies were long and intense.

I started doing really well in school. My father found another woman who was also in the cult and was of Mexican descent. My father remarried and promptly had two sons from that marriage. She was similar to my mother in temperament, though on antidepressants and apparently jealous of my accomplishments. I was the proverbial stepchild. Her children from her previous marriage weren't doing as well. They were degenerates: running away, doing drugs, fighting with their mother. It was horribly difficult because it reminded me of where I had come from.

I completely enmeshed myself into school to escape home. I was national honor society, captain of the dance team, madrigals, swing choir, dance camp, and my favorite thing was musicals. I was part of the student government. I became a rather enigmatic leader in a very short amount of time. I helped coordinate our proms for three years.

Then came the news that my mother was going to die of cancer. I went to see her, though I had decided that I wouldn't ever go back after being thrown out. I had to see her because she was my mom, and I knew she was going to die. She had remarried and was going through chemo. It was awful. My mom told me also that The Way ministry was a cult, and that I really should be careful about "those religious weirdos." When I returned from that visit I stopped going to my dad's "meetings." It was okay though; my father never forced anything on me.

His wife, though, wasn't happy. That was where they had met, and I became their bone of contention. At one point my stepmother punched me in the face and broke a picture of me in the hallway. I went to school the next day to inform them of the assault. The school reacted immediately. Our family had to attend family counseling, and from that point forward it was a civil war that my stepmother ultimately won.

I was kicked out of the home by my stepmom one month before my graduation, and I moved in with my boyfriend's parents. They took care of me until I graduated, and I did graduate with honors. My mother had passed, and I ended up with her car. I was also led to a good job at Resort Condominiums International with the help of my new "family." My stepmother's anger was then turned towards my baby brother, and I rescued him. When I went to pick up my brother, there were bruises all around his neck. I called my oldest sister who immediately bought him a plane ticket back home to Nashville. My sister then took over as "mom" again. In retrospect, she had always been our mother. My brother began high school under my sister's care. He also had swollen lymph nodes, and my sister took him around to every specialist that she could find in Nashville. Another year passed, and his condition was described as "normal" for a boy his age. I took all of us on a vacation to Florida with my benefits from work. When we were in Florida together for our first real sibling vacation, I told my sister that I thought that he had cancer, and we should fly him back to Daddy as soon as possible to let him check him out. We did so, and when Daddy came out of the operating room, he said that it was fourth stage Hodgkin's disease and that if my brother died it was all my fault. My father and his team set to work on my brother with new technology that they had gathered, and my brother is still in remission to this day.

I moved back to Nashville from Indianapolis to go to school at Belmont in 1987. I met my first husband, who was directing one of the shows there. He was seven years older than me and could buy alcohol. We drank and did a bunch of drugs together, including ecstasy, pot, mushrooms, cocaine, but mostly alcohol. He was an actor, so I followed him around after I drank myself out of school. I ended up getting lots of cool parts in different theatres throughout Nashville. I worked at the Children's Theatre professionally in Jungle Book, Mother Hicks, and various other plays. I also got an agent and started doing singing telegrams around Nashville with my newest drug buddies who ran their own company. It was a wild time. I also made money as a kissing wench at the Tennessee Renaissance Festival which had just started.

My first husband and I found a place on Love Circle in Nashville. It was a bungalow built into the side of the mountain. It was filled with mold because of the run off from rain. It was cheap and flimsy, but we just didn't care: we were young and in love. He asked me to marry him, and I said yes without hesitation. I always said yes. I had been engaged to my first boyfriend, it never occurred to me to say no.

We married in 1989, and in 1990 I moved to Atlanta to try my acting there. One week after the move to Atlanta I landed a national TV guest-starring role on "In The Heat of the Night." In one week I had landed a huge role, and I began filming within the month. I had found a place to live in Grant Park, and I had found an agent, and my first guest-starring role, all within one month of moving. My husband stayed in Nashville because he was still working at the Children's

Theatre. When we all sat around the TV to watch the episode I was in, my sister told me that my husband was "jealous." Sisters are rarely wrong.

My husband then quit his job and moved to Atlanta with me, though he wasn't pulling his weight. I began working more and not eating much. At one point I didn't eat or sleep for three days. I had a nervous breakdown. I was institutionalized for the first time.

They said it was a psychotic breakdown because I started hearing voices and imagining the end of the world. My husband called my sister, and they had me incarcerated in my first rehab at Charter Peachford mental hospital in Atlanta. When I was released, my husband started taking me to my group therapy classes and making sure that I took my medicine. All it really did was piss me off. I was basically a zombie in my early twenties. I asked him for a divorce and packed up my car and left Atlanta to run back home to my sister. I didn't want to face anything.

Chapter 6

Mrs. Bojangles

I met a woman named Bojangles
and she danced for you
in worn out shoes
Silver hair, ragged shirt
and baggy pants,
that old soft shoe
She'd jump so high,
she'd jump so high,
and she lightly touched down
Mrs. Bojangles, Mrs. Bojangles, dance.

I met her in a cell in New Orleans,
I was down and out
She looked to me to be the eye of age
as she spoke right out
She talked of life, she talked of life,
she laughed, slapped her leg a step
Mrs. Bojangles, Mrs. Bojangles, dance.

She said her name Bojangles and she danced a lick across the cell
She grabbed her pants for a better stance, oh she jumped so high and she
clicked her heels.
She let go laugh, she let go laugh, shook back her clothes all around
Mrs. Bojangles, Mrs. Bojangles, dance.

She danced for those at minstrel shows and county fairs throughout the south
She spoke with tears of 15 years of how her dog and she just travelled all about
Her dog up and died, he up and died, and after 20 years she still grieves
Mr. Bojangles, Mr. Bojangles, dance.

She said I dance now at every chance at honky-tonks for drinks and tips
But most of the time I spend behind these county bars, 'cause I drink's a bit
She shook her head, and as she shook her head, I heard someone ask him, please
Mrs. Bojangles, Mrs. Bojangles, dance

51

January 2009. Thirty days of inpatient care. I stayed . . . some women didn't. I would go out on long walks with my counselor, Jackie. Fresh air brought a new perspective. Jackie was a musician who had played for Jenna Bush's wedding -- yes, the President of the United States' daughter. Coincidence? I don't think so. We spoke about my music and her music. We shared our lives with each other. Jackie was a large black woman with over twenty years of recovery. She was intimidating, honest, funny; and she and God saved my life. I became determined to try something different. I no longer wanted to be my mother. I wanted to be a new mother, a new daughter, a new wife.

Inside we were given group therapy. The most powerful one for me was the rope maze. Forty women, each blindfolded, were led into a large room with a rope maze. We were instructed to find our way out. I was one of the last out. I could hear the others giggling on the side. I kept trying to find my way out. It was dark. I knew that I was backtracking. I could feel the ropes. In desperation, I finally raised my hand. A counselor came to me and whispered in my ear, "is there something you need?" I said, "I don't think there's a way out, I need help!" She said "that's the way out!"

I fell in a heap on the floor. I had been asking for help my whole life, but no one in my family seemed to be able to help. Today I have all sorts of people around me that recognize that growing up means asking for help. It takes courage to do this.

On the last day of rehab, my husband showed up with our van, and of course the divorce. My husband took everything: my house, my baby girl, and my freedom. But, in spite of it all, I stayed sober. My God continued working for me 24 hours a day, seven days a week. My early recovery included two halfway house stays and some time in a battered women's homeless shelter. I was quantifiably homeless for eight months. I stayed sober throughout all of it. Rehab gave me the tools, and I started using them every day.

On January 21st 2009, my daughter Cecilia wrote:

I never knew drinking was bad until the night of January 21st 2009. That night changed my life and my sister's life forever. It started just like any other night. I was upstairs online on Myspace, listening to music, when I heard screaming between my mom and step-dad. That is what was normal in my house. My mom was trying to teach my little sister her vocabulary words for kindergarten. My step-dad was drunk and shoving a digital recorder in my mom's face. He was saying "Mama don't like being recorded." My mom had also been drinking earlier in the day. I started hearing pans banging, and I went downstairs to get my little sister away from the oncoming trouble. I didn't want my sister to see them shouting at each other or fighting again.

I guess my mom jumped on my step-dad and scratched his face enough for it to break the skin and bleed. Then there was no noise. No screaming, no pans clanging. I was afraid because I had a dream that my step-father had shot my mom before. Our home was not a peaceful place.

I was trying to show my sister how to play a game on the computer upstairs when I saw blue lights filling up the room. I heard car doors, and I jumped to the window and saw two cops: they were knocking on our door. They weren't inside long by the time I came downstairs, and then they were locking my mom up in the back of their car. They had my mom in handcuffs. My step dad was coming upstairs, so I jumped on the futon and held my baby sister close.

When he walked in, his face looked no different from any other day except the blood. He didn't look scared or even distressed, just numb as usual. I started looking at his facial features. He had a scratch from the corner of his eye to

the end of his chin and another scratch right next to it, but
not severe. He was bleeding, and it looked like it would drip
off his chin.

My husband came home from war, and he brought both the war and a new affair home with him. I had taken care of our home and our children during his two eighteen-month deployments. It took me two years to plan our wedding, and it took him nine months to destroy our family.

January 21st 2009, I woke up in jail. Curled up on a concrete slab in a very tiny holding cell in Wilson County with a toilet. It was similar to the whole marriage. Trapped like a rat. I cried myself to sleep, but before I slept, I cried out to God for help.

I started walking back home after calling my sister, who had taken care of the bond. It was weird how warm that day was when I reached my final point of desperation. I knew I was becoming my mother -- an alcoholic. Lost in my bottles, hiding them, disappearing into my "writing room." Totally alone. A stay-at-home drunk. I picked up an old cigarette on the side of the road to smoke. There were holes in the back of my ankles from walking. The dried blood of my husband was underneath my nails. I kept walking and wondering how had

I turned into such a weird, tired, little animal. I had been going to school at MTSU to become an elementary education teacher. I had been on the parent-teacher organization helping my daughter's school get their new sign. I'd even presented my husband with the key to the city of Lebanon for his service. God? Please help me. But God answers prayers in crooked lines.

A woman stopped her car at about mile number five to give me a ride. She was kind. God immediately started sending human angels to scoop me up and carry me. She was the first. She asked me where I was going, and I started crying again and told her through my snot about the assault. I told her that I was hopeful that my husband wouldn't want to shoot me when I arrived.

She put her hand on my shoulder and said that she had been attending the little church close by our home for twenty years, and that sometimes there are just things missing in our lives. I didn't understand her at that point.

At home, my husband was screaming that if the police knew that I was there, I would be arrested. The phone rang. My sister was on the line telling me that she would be able to get me into rehab, if I wanted help. At first I said no, I could get sober on my own. Then I said yes. I started packing a bag of clothes and left, while my husband screamed behind me. His voice was beyond description; really the decibel levels most likely could have busted our ear drums.

I gave both of my babies a kiss and told them that Mama was going to go and get some help. I went to a nasty hotel and slept. I went to my first meeting of hope the next evening. That circle pointed me to another circle the next night. My hands were sweaty, my body was shaking from detoxing, but I made it one night without alcohol.

I met a circle of women who gave me a card with their phone numbers on it, and it said "If things never changed, there wouldn't be butterflies." I picked a woman named Cathy to call, and she was the one I started calling every single night. I was three days sober when I was admitted to Cumberland Heights. My sister and my brother-in-law took care of the bill, and I began to finally get a little rest and some medical help for the amount of trauma that I had endured my whole life.

I started with a group of seven women. Lawyers, nurses, house moms: seriously smart ladies who couldn't outsmart their addictions. In the morning, we would gather with our counselor, Jackie, to begin to learn how to acknowledge and identify our "feelings." I wasn't sure when I had ever done this before.

Feelings? Really? How the hell is this supposed to help me?

Chapter 7
Running

Been fighting demons
in the middle of the night.
Clinging to my soul
in the morning light.
I've been running....
I've been running...

Looking for love on the outside
I aint enough to keep me alive
I've been running
I've been running

Oh, the past is black as coal
These chains of shame
don't work no more.
Only God really knows
There's no peace in my soul
Til' I just let go and stop this
Running...
Gotta stop running...

Putting on the gloves
and ready for a fight
Release the rage to realize
Gotta stop running
Gotta stop running

Oh, the past is black as coal
These chains of shame
don't work no more.
Only God really knows
There's no peace in my soul
Til' I just let go and stop this
Running...
Gotta stop running...

February 2009. Prior to being released from inpatient treatment, I was counseled that I needed serious ongoing therapy and a safe place to stay. I was directed to a licensed clinical therapist. She specialized in post-traumatic stress disorders and EMDR therapy. I moved into a women's half way house in Nashville and got a job at Krystal as a cashier. It was weird: my resume included executive secretarial experience. The manager who interviewed me was perplexed. She wanted to know why I was trying to get a job at a fast food restaurant when I had experience such as this. My response was "I just need a job."

The halfway house was huge, old, blue, and filled with other ladies like myself, all trying to change their lives. I learned from each one of them. We had a schedule of chores to be done each night. We had a set amount of outside group therapy we had to go to each week. We had to follow all of the rules or be asked to leave with a 15-minute window. I couldn't give out my address to anyone for the safety of the other women. I learned from the ladies. I learned about DC4, which is a drug court program. My friend Nicki had drunk Draino at Walmart and survived. She was only one of thirteen people in the whole world that had survived this kind of suicide attempt. It was a bad day at Walmart. We were tight. I learned from an older lady that morning was the time for "spiritual food." I started working, and when I got my first paycheck, I cried. It was the first full-time job that I had since my total isolation had begun after the marriage in 2002.

I also had my first spiritual experience at work. I was making the coffee in the morning for the breakfast crew when in one-half of a second a weird shadow popped out of my body. I saw it. It was like the shadow from Peter Pan, no kidding. The shadow ran off so quickly, and I knew that it was a very small piece of the terror from my childhood popping out and being released.

EMDR therapy is like trying to unravel old terror from the past. It is stuck in your brain. It's like your brain isn't breathing or something. You put headphones on which beep back and forth and hold buzzing balls in each hand as you walk back in time through the trauma. It's intense. What it does is it releases all of the old deadened feelings and creates a balance in your brain to allow you to just go through feelings and move forward. The farther back the trauma occurred, the longer that it takes. Mine began at eleven years old, so it took us two years of work, but I was determined. I knew that my mother's poor choices had affected my poor choices as an adult. I wanted the cycle of abuse to end once and for all.

Trauma is released sideways: it came out as anger and a whole bunch of that was directed at my husband at that time.

My husband was busy with his paperwork. I was busy getting a new circle of friends. Though they didn't last long. In fact, during two of our house meetings, they turned on me. I was told that they had found a bottle of unopened rum on the back porch, and that they all thought it was my husband who had set it there. I didn't really know if that was the case. I didn't have much contact with him. Any kind of alcohol or drug was prohibited for obvious reasons. They kicked me out of the house after a "hen pecking party" when I had only been there for two months. Nicki was the only woman who stood up for me.

I left. I called my spiritual guide. She asked, "did you stay sober?" I said, "Yes." She said, "Well then, there's hope, and you have to find another safe place to stay." So I spent one night at my cousin's house, but they weren't safe for me because of the alcohol in their home. I found another place the next evening, when I went to The Freedom House. Franny was the next angel that God brought to me. Franny had known me prior to the horrific marriage. She made a few phone calls, and more women came to give me a safe place, called The Women of Worth house. There I had a bunk bed in the basement with six other women who had come out of prison. I continued getting on my knees in the morning and at night. I continued going to work at Krystal and even started going to Krystal Kollege (yes that's with a K) to raise my pay up a dime and show the court that I was trying to better myself for my children. I had no idea what God had planned, but it was beyond my own comprehension for certain. I met a woman from prison during that time. She taught me that there are therapeutic communities inside the prison systems. She had been incarcerated for four years' time for theft and other felonies. You couldn't see that in her soul. She was a large, motherly figure in the Home. She taught me the meditation that they learned in prison and that we are all born into this world with overflowing potential. I wasn't sure if I would find my potential.

The basement was old enough to have a wall air conditioning unit in it. It leaked. The ladies all piled into my van to go to our group therapy together. It was wild. We were smoking cigarettes, blasting music super loudly, talking about everything, fixing the world together. There was also a basketball goal to play basketball outside. We also had a few cats that we fed and took care of. I made friends with one lady named Krissy who had been a prostitute and had been stabbed multiple time in her chest. The scars were long and bumpy, serious like her eyes. I brought her fishing at Two Rivers Pond one day to talk about her life and her survival skills. As soon as we got back, we were asked to piss in cups, just in case we had been out using drugs or alcohol. I was naive. I didn't realize how hardened some of the other ladies were. They referred to me as their "Flower Child."

I was told that I could stay during the week and go home on the weekend to take care of my home and my children, since it was court- ordered. I was supposed to attend one house meeting a month, and I missed the first one because I was so tired from therapy. They kicked me out because I couldn't move. I found another place after once again calling my spiritual guide and her saying pretty much the same thing. She said, "Did you drink? Well…God has a plan. Bye. I love you."

I spent two nights in my van and kept going to my group therapy and my EMDR therapy. I took a few baths in any sink that I could find at gas stations. I also took a shower in a church before I found shelter again. I guess God's plan included finding myself in a battered women's homeless shelter at exactly the right time.

The next day in court in Wilson County, Judge Gwin decided to give me shelter at the Brooks House Homeless Shelter. It was a miracle. The waiting list there was over six months long. Apparently, the Judge's wife was on the board of directors of the home, and they had a little bit of influence. My husband was determined to use everything that he could against me, though I was unaware of the amount of deceit and underlying lies that he was collecting. It didn't matter, I stayed sober.

The judge once again let me go home on the weekends to take care of my home and my children. The summer of 2009 was glorious. My children and I played croquet on every weekend. We cooked up big home-made meals. I made an amends to my oldest one night after being five minutes late from my group therapy. She called me in fear, "Mama, where are you?" I heard her fear. I said, "I'm at the Piggly Wiggly, and I will be home in a few minutes." When I came home, she was shaking and said that she thought I was going to stop off at the liquor store just like I had done so many times before. I wrapped her shaking little tiny body into mine and told her, "Baby, I am really going to try this thing this time." I stayed sober; my husband didn't.

The divorce came in September of 2009. My brother and sister gave me a place to stay at the Hotel Preston for two weeks prior to the divorce. It is a 4-Star hotel. I had gone from being quantifiably homeless for eight whole months to a 4-Star hotel, and as soon as the divorce was final, it was time to pack.

Chapter 8
Grace & Gravity

Woke up restless as the sun,
feeling Grandma's Cherokee blood.
Made up a bed filled with guilt and shame
Where you and I made our baby's name

Chorus:
Oh grace and gravity please be kind to me

Woke up lying to the moon,
feeling battered broken and bruised,
from a man's lies and the same man's fears
He can't control my life he can't hold back my tears

Chorus:
Oh grace and gravity please keep my spirit free

Bridge:
Big wheel keep moving on,
Crown Victoria point me and my babies home
Woke up shining like the sun,
swollen eyes crying all done
A new day dawns on the shoulder of the road
My babies cry, but Mama has hope that grace and gravity
Will keep her babies free and grace and gravity will keep their Mama free

September 2009. I got an apartment back in Nashville. My husband took my home, and he also took my baby girl Jenessa. My baby was in kindergarten and had to take kindergarten again because of the divorce. She was very angry. I was cut off from being her mother. I was also angry, but mostly angry at myself for thinking that there was stability in the marriage.

We packed up the home in four hours' time with four men from my home group. I had no idea that God would be able to coordinate an actual moving crew for me that day, but He certainly did. My oldest daughter was elated to see our whole house being unpacked from that truck that day! She was overwhelmed with relief to be finally free from the hell hole that we had lived in. To this day we refer to Wilson County as "The Hell Hole."

I asked Miss Liz Reese if she would help me to get into Belmont which has one of the most prestigious music business programs in the nation. Miss Liz wrote the letter of recommendation for me to attend. I didn't even have a computer. I wrote my essay long-hand, and it basically said that it would be important for my oldest daughter Cecilia, who was just twelve at that time, to see her mother go through something traumatic and move forward with footwork and with faith and pop out the other side stronger and smarter. I got in. It was unbelievable!

My husband had been telling my youngest daughter Jenessa that I "was just going to school" when I was living in the battered women's homeless shelter. Apparently, God has a sense of humor and must have decided that it was actually a great idea.

January 2011. My husband was drunk as usual and threatening to kill the neighbor's dog next door with his hand gun. I got word through my old neighbors about the new drunken dramatic behaviors. I made sure that I took the filed written complaint that showed that my husband had been also threatening to kill the dog while a teenager was holding her dog's neck and begging for the life of her family pet. The girlfriend was still in the picture at that time, and she begged and pleaded profusely with the neighbors to not press charges against her boyfriend. I should have gotten my baby girl back from the ex then, but somehow the enablers continue to rescue him. I also found out that the ex-husband also had called the Wilson County Sherriff's to the home on seven different times during a three-month span. I wasn't sure how anyone could miss this obvious PTSD.

My now ex-husband and I continued arguing via emails; one email in particular clearly threatened my life. I took that email to the Davidson County courts and got a restraining order against him. He was ordered at that time to turn in his gun for six months' time. In response to the order of protection, my ex-husband used the courts in Wilson County to take away *all of my parental rights!*

I was a single, sober mother in Nashville (I had one baby, my oldest, living with me), I was working, and I was going to school at Belmont. The court systems in the Wilson County good-ole-boy judicial system apparently do not acknowledge the obvious. I was only able to see my baby girl at supervised visits, and those cost me $20.00 each hour, every other weekend. My baby girl began to be rather distanced and filled with many nights of crying for her mommy.

My ex-mother-in-law took over the duties of my job as Jenessa's mother. She went as far as to buy a new home in Lebanon, Tennessee, and move from South Georgia, using all of their retirement money to do so. It is amazing what happens when families are in denial of the truth. My ex-mother-in-law is also an adult child of an alcoholic, and she is still in denial that her son is an alcoholic. It is wildly obvious of course, now that he has another alcoholic who has three children from three different failed relationships. The cycle continues.

My ex-husband also went as far as he could go within the judicial system in Wilson County. Judge Gwinn was furious when he point-blank asked my ex-husband in court, "Do you want me to put her in jail for a year?!!" It became rather obvious by my ex-husband's non-response that he did. I was arrested for Contempt of Court in 2011. During that time, I served three days in jail for his newest charges. I was arrested once again six months later, and at that time I appealed the whole case to the Supreme Court system in Davidson County. A real judicial system would be able to figure things out. I was still considered indigent at that time, and the courts in Wilson County had to hire an appeals attorney for me. Her name was Andrea Hagen, and she was one scary, smart, sharp lady. She walked like a soldier and extended her arm in a handshake like a willowy man. Andrea and I worked together to decipher the mess of alcoholism in our response and research the pending possible incarceration.

I had ninety-seven days hanging over my head, and I was still trying to stay focused at Belmont. I was also coordinating a fundraising event for the Brooks House homeless shelter as a class project for my music publishing class with Dan Keen.

Thankfully, my professors at Belmont surrounded me at that time and kept me focused.

October of 2011. My ex-husband showed up at Belmont on his knees, next to my car. I didn't know what he wanted. He said that he was no longer seeing the girlfriend anymore. I gathered that the girl had finally had enough of the obvious and left, for the moment.

I jumped out of the car and stood my ground. I screamed, "I was in a parenting class with three other women who said that their husbands were trying to *kill them*! Does that sound like fun to *you*?" That's when my ex-husband said, "You are sinking further into *your* disease!" My response was, "I am a single parent! You are like a bad penny; you just keep coming back! I am looking at ninety-seven days in jail, dude! That's reality!"

I got into my car and drove away. I called Father Klasic, my other spiritual guide who had married us. His response was, "Is he on drugs? He has been dragging you and your children through the court system for years!" Father Klasic was also one of the folks who wrote a letter of recommendation for Belmont. He said, "Lois, I need for you to do something for me, okay?" I responded, "Okay." Father Klasic said, "I need for you to be grateful for the professors at

77

Belmont for giving an old lady with a bunch a baggage a chance, because it appears as if it is probably going to pay off."

January of 2012. Andrea Hagen, the attorney that Judge Gwin had hired for me, and I uncovered Malicious Judicial Intent within the ex-husband's timing of his use of the Wilson County Judicial system: it was all dismissed. *The whole case dismissed!*

I moved forward with trying my best to get my baby girl back, in court, on my own, and I kept my transcripts from the hearings. I still did not have any monetary help to secure a lawyer from my family. I did end up with the specific instructions from an actual Judge who is also a co-writer friend of mine. I brought in my own transcriptionist for the hearing, as well as a Davidson County Police officer, who also recorded everything that was said during the hearing to keep for records. I was given more time with my baby girl at supervised visits. But I had to continue to pay some stranger to sit and watch me be her mother. It wasted another full summer of my time with my baby girl.

My baby girl continued to say that the girl was not living in their home; however, I already knew that would change. People are predictable. We had been divorced in September

2009, and the newest girlfriend was painting my home in November 2009. They only had alcohol and drugs in common. I knew all about that relationship. It was no longer a good look for me. I must have grown a little bit.

I started my own music publishing company, called Sounds Like A Small City. It is the very first women-run music publishing company that is specifically designed to change the life of another woman. Along with my friend and confidant, Khang Tran Tran, a man who was a Harvard graduate and studying for a master's degree in entrepreneurial studies at Belmont, I pieced together the first executive plan to launch the company.

Chapter 9
I've Seen Too Much to Give Up Now

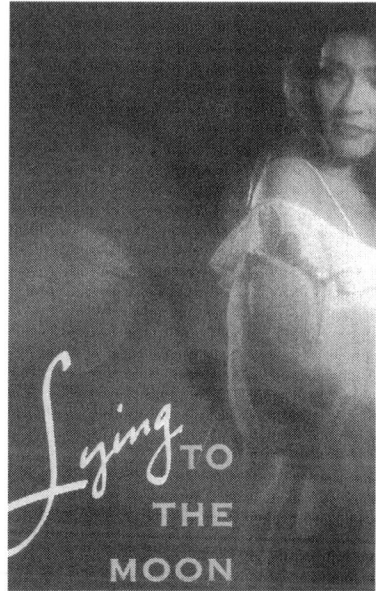

Snowed under the washed out sky,
face down in the quiet tears I cry
When the path disappeared.
I know Jesus he's my friend
but I'm too tired to talk it out again
On my knees I'm still here.
Could you break the ice?
Cause I'm wearing thin,
can I still find strength
And remember when

Chorus:
I've seen too much love in the world,
I've seen too much love in the world.
I've seen too much love to give up now.
I've seen so much grace in the world.
Trying to find my place in the world,
I've seen too much love to give up now.
To give up now.

Drifting further in a deep blue sea,
almost drowning
in the darkest side of me,
Looking for love deeper still.
You didn't part the waves or set the sky on fire,
just a whisper came but I heard a thousand choirs.

Repeat Chorus

Bridge:
I've seen things that I don't understand
and I can't change out of my hands
and though my heart is broken, it's still beating,
it's wide open yeah..it's wide open yeah yeah

81

March 2011. Belmont College is an amazing music business hub for furthering an educational understanding of the music and entertainment industry. I was lucky to be surrounded by some of the brightest and most ambitious students at that time. During my studies in my music publishing class, we were required to have a class project of choosing an artist to legally publish their music as well as creating a live performance of the album's release. I ended up with nine students on my "love pod" team. Dan Keen was the professor for that particular class. He has years of experience within the music publishing business in Nashville. He is one of my cheerleaders to this day, as well as a good friend of mine now.

I remember the very first day of class, going around the room and introducing ourselves, at which point one student, a girl, said that her interests were in learning more about women's social issues. I gave that girl a brochure for the Brooks House, which spawned the idea to not only publish my music, but also to host a fundraising event for the Brooks House at The Curb Music Café at Belmont. It became a huge success for us, and we also ended up being able, with Miss Liz Reese's help, to bring the ladies from the shelter to the event. Miss Liz said that when I was a student at Belmont, they had called her on the phone to inquire as to whether or not my story was true. We hosted the event in April, and the women that came to the event were filled with true hope, because they all knew that I had been in their shoes. I wrote a song for Miss Liz called *Mama,* which is what we refer to her at the Brooks House. The Lebanon Democrat newspaper covered the event and wrote the article I've included below.

My sister Matraca gave me this other song that fits my description of my life during this time, called *I've Seen Too Much Love To Give Up Now.* It describes in detail musically how lost my path had become after no longer being a mother and a wife. I can say without a doubt that I must be pretty much the luckiest singer / songwriter in Nashville today to have her as my mentor.

Giving back: Former Brooks House resident plans concert to benefit shelter

By MARY E. HINDS, Staff Writer

In a classic case of what goes around comes around, a former resident of Brooks House is taking measures to help the organization that helped her.

Lois Berg, a singer, song writer and musician who is poised to make her mark in Nashville, is planning a

84

concert Saturday, April 16, at the Curb Music Cafe on the campus of Belmont University. Donations at the concert will benefit Brooks House. The concert begins at 7 p.m. Admission is free, but there will be donations boxes near the stage so the audience can contribute to the shelter. Her CD will be on sale for $10 with $5 of that going to Brooks House. Other Belmont students will be performing at the show as well.

Berg spent four months at Brooks House, the Lebanon shelter for women and children in crisis, when she was going through a traumatic divorce. The people at Brooks House helped Berg get her life back together, and she has moved on to pursue a brighter future. After leaving Brooks House, Berg went on to Belmont University, where she is now a senior.

Director Liz Reese, who is called "Mama" by Brooks House residents, is thrilled to have one of the program's brightest stars back in the fold.

"She wants to give back to the Brooks House, where she got focused and was able to get back on her feet. She is one of our biggest success stories," Reese said. "I want to bring this to light so people can see it doesn't matter what you're going through; if you've got your head on right, you can succeed."

Reese certainly sounds like a proud Mama when talking about Berg.

"Lois was full of life and very humorous. When she said 'I think I'm going to go back to school' I said that's what you need to do, find something to focus on. She's a wonderful musician with a beautiful voice. That's where she is now, going to school and working on her music. We're really excited about it."

Berg gives the women of Brooks House full credit for helping her put her life back on track.

"They gave me food and shelter during a really dark time in my life. I had to go through a divorce, and during the divorce they gave me a place to stay where I could basically regenerate myself and get back on my feet," Berg said. "Miss Liz wrote the recommendation that helped get me into Belmont."

Reese says the women who find themselves at Brooks House become a family and most look to support one another.

"People say the girls leave and they don't do anything, but that's not true. They always want to come back and encourage the ladies who are here. They want to come back and help — whatever Mama needs. Those are the most important things we look for and everybody doesn't have that, but every now and then you get that diamond that's going to sparkle. That's what I see in Lois," Reese added. "On any given day I see at least one or two former residents, because this is home for them. Some leave and don't ever come back, but then there are those who want to be supportive. They need the guidance, the communication and they just need to be loved on. When they get in a hard situation, all children come back home in some form or fashion. When you have those who come back to give back, that's the most important thing."

Berg's biographical press release describes her as "a force of nature, a chronicler of life and midwife of dreams whose music meets at the corner of real country and modern art." She is the daughter of a nuclear physicist and a coal miner's daughter, who is finding her feet in the business of modern country music. She has performed around the country and is part of a worldwide compilation album released through www.Gogirlsmusic.com. Her new album, "White Trash

Cookbook," is a stripped-down production that puts no barriers between the artist and the listener.

The April 16 concert came about because of a class project Berg was working on with two fellow student musicians at Belmont.

"We were all talking about the show. One of the students in the group is interested in social issues, and I told her it would be super cool if we could invite some of the ladies of Brooks House, and she suggested we make it a fundraiser," Berg said. "I jumped on that like a Texan on a pork chop."

She also jumped at the opportunity to give back to the program that sheltered her when she was at a low point in her life.

"These girls come in and they're broken, they're scared and they feel alone. Then they grow into the bond of a family. They may go on their merry way, but they don't forget where they came from and what has gotten them through the hard times," Reese said. Lois was so full of life and bubbly, and she always said she wanted to do something for Brooks House, because she learned something here."

What Berg learned is how to give back, and Brooks House can only benefit from that lesson learned.

"It's like a dream, but I'm wide awake," Berg said with a laugh.

Chapter 10
Mama

Ooooo, oooooo, ooooo ahhh
Mama told me as a little girl, life is a dream in a simple world
God has a plan, for beauty and grace and I hope you learn from my mistakes
Chorus:
You don't need my wings to fly, you can hold your head up high
You can walk through a wall of lies, you don't have to be afraid of life.
Mama she told me
Bridge: bruises heal with time, mama said, and a diamond you will find in the
darkest coal mine. Hold on to your faith, your wings will grow baby just you
wait.
Mama she told me
Mama told me as a young lady, your love will be strong for your babies
God has a plan, for their beauty and grace…you will have to let them learn from
their mistakes.
Chorus: they don't need your wings to fly, they can hold their heads up high
They can walk through a wall of lies, they don't have to be afraid of life.
Mama she told me, mama aaaahaaaaa she told me, I don't need her wings to fly

May 2011: I wrote *Mama* in honor of the many mamas in my life, specifically Miss Liz Reese, who is the director of the Brooks House Homeless shelter in Lebanon, TN.

My mama always told me that "I could do anything I set my mind to." Even though my mother could not produce a home that was stable for us as children, she still gave me a glimpse of what determination looked like. Her mother, my grandmother, must of also instilled a few life giving survival skills in her. My grandmother, Icie Calloway, also has quite an amazing story of exactly how she followed the train tracks as a child to run from her slavery and miraculously find her sister.

When Icie Calloway, my grandmother in Harlan County, Kentucky, turned ninety-seven years old, the Calloway family decided that we would all gather in the holler to celebrate her years on the earth.

During that time my sister, Matraca, was keeping close contact with the ex-husband; she went to rescue my baby girl for the weekend. It was the very first time since 2009 that my children and I were together for a weekend without my ex-husband threatening me with courts, lawyers and Judges.

It's fairly easy for mamas to detect when their babies are unhappy. It took a few days for her to perk up. We began the family pilgrimage back home to the oldest living matriarch of our family. The peace and serenity of the mountains of Harlan County, Kentucky, still brings me memories of wild fun filled days as a child. Fishing, swimming and climbing the mountains together with my cousins. It is as if time had still not touched the beauty and the simple life there. I am eternally grateful today, though, that my mother followed my Aunt Sudie to Nashville. I know that I would not have been able to accomplish half of the things that I have managed to move towards as an adult if she'd stayed in Harlan County.

It's a beautiful place to visit, but I sure wouldn't want to live there. The TV dishes are bigger than some of the trailers that are in the holler.

Icie Calloway may be fragile, however, she is still quite a sharp lady of faith. The drive to Harlan was and always will be a pilgrimage back into history. My lungs filled once again with that pure mountain air and memories of my childhood. We made it back home to where my mother had been raised. The family all came together for a weekend filled with food, music and love. I held my baby girl as close as I could for a few sweet moments in time; by now she'd grown so much it was difficult to even remember when she was little. I got as many pictures of her at that time as I could. We went swimming and fishing with my cousins in the backwaters of the Cumberland. Sunday morning, I brought the children to the Baptist church in Harlan where my grandma had brought me as a child. The music and the message was still the same. The preacher was also the same, screaming hell and heaven, golden sidewalks for those believers of "JESUS!" My grandmother had asked me, "Well, little Lois, what'd you think of the sermon?" My response was, "He gave me a headache." "Well," Granny said, "that's just the way he gets his message across." My daughters both had the same response as I had that morning. I was filled with joy and happiness at that moment. I was home. I put five dollars into the donation basket and took the advice of one of the elders in the church. His advice was that "You kiss your children on the heads and bless them with your presence. Then you let God take care of your children because HE WILL take care of all of his children!"

As I walked out of the little church that had brought me a few moments of history, one of my cousins followed me out to my car. My cousin knew my Mama, and she said that, "You remind me so much of your mother. Monk was so scattered and brilliantly funny." She wanted to buy some of my CD's. She bought five of my CD's for $10 each. I had put $5 in the donation basket at the little Baptist Church in Harlan County, and God blessed me with $50, plus now there were some of my family in Harlan that were listening to my music! It gave me hope to know that I had come home and was able to leave a little bit of my mother's dreams up there in the holler of Harlan County.

I had also brought my guitar along with me, and my sister used it to serenade my Grandma Calloway. My sister is a legend up there now because she co-wrote *Strawberry Wine*, and she is a three-time Grammy-nominated singer songwriter. She is the youngest songwriter to ever be placed into the Songwriter's Hall of Fame!

I have some serious legendary musical roots in my family, my namesake Lois Johnson had duets with Hank Williams Junior. My step father Dave Kirby wrote for Merle Haggard and penned *Is Anyone Going to San Antone.*" I have tried to give up on my music but it's just part of my bone marrow structure, like beans and cornbread. I get pulled right back into it. Now I have a few folks around me as well that will not let me give up on my music. God knows more about what is going to occur in my life today.

I didn't know it at that time, but my car was about to die on me, and it was the very last thing that I had left that reminded me of the broken home I had left in Wilson County. My sister and my brother-in-law were bringing my youngest daughter back to my ex when my car died that day. It's a miracle that my brother-in-law had decided to go the same route as I. Once again, my sister came to my rescue and purchased a car for me.

I guess when you end up with hit country songs over a period of time you have a few checks that can buy a car or two for your family members. When we walked into Carmax, I felt like a contestant on The Price Is Right!! "Lois, come on down!! Here's your new car!!" I was screaming like a wild Price Is Right contestant!! "Yeeehawww ya'll." One moment it appeared as if I would have to be riding the bus when my car melted down on the highway; the next day it was replaced with a brand new, shiny car from my sister. It gave me the ability to get to classes on time and to begin to wrap up my credits at Belmont. My sister, who only got a GED for her education, had purchased me and my oldest daughter a brand new vehicle! It was just one of the wildest most amazing days of my life because of the number of struggles that I had already gone through.

So the path of being married and being a mother had disappeared, but it no longer mattered. I could learn how to love myself again, and I no longer had to give up hope for a better life. Thank God for sisters who are older and wiser and become more like mothers because of past struggles. Thank God, especially, for gifted sisters and that blood is always thicker than water. Today I am co-writing a new song with my sister called *California*. It is the story about my wild days in my twenties when I drove across the country in my '87 Chevy Chevette. Here's my sister's website for y'all. www.matracaberg.com.

Chapter 11

Crooked Lines

He was moving slow like watching a swimmer in a pool of honey
Barely moving from the night before.
He kept on drinking I kept on thinking it'd all be over
But he's still drunk and I'm stone cold sober.

The lights were low and the music loud
He fell off a barstool and stumbled through the crowd
Put his rugged hand at the small of my back ooooooo two stepping heart attack

Chorus:
crooked lines crooked teeth crooked wild child underneath
crooked man with a complex mind I slipped and fell between your crooked lies

I'm a straight shooter that fell between his crooked lines
Thought he was smooooooth but he's doctor Jekyl Mr. Hyde

Chorus:
Crooked lines crooked teeth crooked wild child underneath
Crooked man with a complex mind I slipped and fell between your crooked lies

July 2016. Co-parenting came a tiny bit easier after having help from Conflict Resolution Center in Nashville. That was in the year 2014. I finally got my weekends with my daughter and began to reestablish my relationship with her. My oldest was super excited to have her baby sister back in her life on a regular basis. We had, we thought, gone through all of the lies and popped out on the other side. We were wrong.

I moved to a home in Old Hickory and got a roommate from Saudi Arabia. My ex decided that because he was from Saudi Arabia, he was going to sell our daughter as a child bride. Christmas that year included the police on my front porch. Thankfully I had gotten in touch with a man who was an attorney at that time, and he was able to begin to stick up for me and my girls. My roommate was actually just a student going to school in the United States to become a respiratory therapist. He was also a musician and helped me to produce a really neat song called *Angels along the Way*.

I was working at a day-care at the City Road United Methodist Church when my ex called me with his news about my roommate being a terrorist. He had even gone so far as to send me some horrific CNN news links from the internet. My response was, "she's twelve, I've got a feeling that she's not going to be married anytime soon. When she does get married

101

it will probably be in the United States, but that's just a guess."

I assume my ex had even "convinced" his parents of this ludicrous lie, and he wanted me to call his mom to explain. I told him that "It sounds to me like your PTSD is flaring up, and no thanks, I don't feel like I need to communicate with your parents about my visits with my daughter."

Me and my daughter were at the movies when my roommate texted me the weird news about my ex and the police on my front porch. My daughter was immediately filled with fear and I got online to reach out for help from my buddy and senior pastor at the church to find a safe place to sleep. My pastor asked my daughter the only question that really mattered, "Are you being held against your will?" "Of course not," she answered.

We enjoyed our time together while my ex went on ahead and got in touch with his attorney, and it became yet another "buy someone to sit and watch me and my oldest daughter visit." Thankfully we only did this for just a few short weeks. My daughter wasn't happy about it at all, because by now she really understood exactly what was going on. Once again, I had to kick out my roommate and start over fresh. It's like living my life in someone else's fear. Though of course without all of this conflict, I wouldn't have so many new songs and stories for my children to learn from. I'm always looking on the bright side. Though it all still baffles me today just how much drama one person can create without conscious thoughts.

We finally got a court ordered parenting plan. That only took us seven years.

Then came the worst news we had ever gotten. He decided that he would move to Florida, eight hours away. We were just a few months from finally having a real parenting plan, and now the guy and the new girlfriend were running off with my baby girl to Florida.

His weird letter included a slew of lies about my daughter wanting to learn about "fish," when in reality, my daughter is probably less interested in fish than anyone I know. Here's what I know about her: she's a mini-me. She's a beyond-talented singer, and of course from just this tiny bit of information y'all have, y'all can imagine what kind of opportunities await her.

My answer was an emphatic, "No!!" My attorney and I immediately began to work on the "newest" opposition to the run. My daughter had been telling me about this for a few months prior to all of this upheaval. She had already been moved to five different schools within seven years. The amount of instability in that alone would surely keep this horrific event from happening.

I had to seek outside help for this additional trauma and thankfully, once again, my sister came to my rescue. I started more therapy to prepare for yet more trauma. It was and still is unbelievable to me. The new couple did their very best to put on this weird show. Prior to the new court hearing, the new soon-to-be wife "pretended" like it was going to be great. Yeah, it sounds great alright. Not in a million years does it sound great.

So the interrogations began again, and by this point I had gotten a job at Vanderbilt; a really nice job that could have given me and my children everything we needed to break free. Once again though, because of the impending doom, I couldn't concentrate, and I was fired right before we went back to court.

It's kind of weird now looking back on it. The newest video I had released, called *Vavavoom*, must have been viewed by the Sherriff and the Judge. When I walked back into the Wilson County Family Court system that year, they remembered me. In fact, the guy said, "Hey, Lois. Where you been?" I said, "Graduated from Belmont, the ex wants to run off to Florida." I have no clue why I married that guy. Still don't. I wasn't sure if that was a good sign that they remembered me, or a bad sign. Guess it doesn't really matter today. All I know is that my God still works for me, and I will fight for my baby girls until there's no breath left in me.

Chapter 12
Ripped

Ripped from my body
suckled on my breast
Baby girl your mama's world
will always be blessed
I'm the rock your standing on
every minute of the day
Not my plan out of my hands
they ripped you away

Chorus:
There's a hole empty and black,
years of time we will never get back
There's a hole empty and black that's
the way it goes til you fly back

Like a butterfly in a hurricane, beauty caught in chaos
I'm the shelter in your rain.

Chorus:
There's a hole empty and black, years of time we will never get back
There's a hole empty and black thats the way it goes til you fly back

Bridge: I've fought for so long to bring you back home. I had to let go again
But even a perfect storm has an end.

Chorus:
There's a hole empty and black, years of time we will never get back
There's a hole empty and black that's the way it goes til you fly back.
Til you fly back

July 2016. The trial was pretty quick. I brought in seven different witnesses; my close friends who had gone through all of it with me. The ex only brought himself and his attorney. Apparently the guy had gotten married a few days prior to the trial and looked pretty much like he was coming off of a three-day binge. I also found out from my daughter that they had been telling her that she couldn't live with me the whole trip back. My daughter kept saying that wasn't true because my oldest had been living with me for years. Manipulating children, I guess, comes pretty easy for these folks.

As soon as my daughter came in, she was shuffled into the Judge's chambers, and she was asked a bunch of questions. I guess the only thing that made the biggest difference was that she said, "I want MORE time with my mom." My oldest daughter also got on the stand that day, and she was such a trooper. I am still proud of her courage and strength. She talked about the amount of alcohol that she watched my ex consume when she went to Florida on vacation with them. The Judge stood up for her as well when she was cross examined.

Nadia Bruce-Rawlings got up on the stand that day to testify on my behalf. It's wild how my story started writing itself just like the majority of my songs do. She made the

Judge laugh whenever she was describing being a step-mom and how it's not exactly a bed of roses.

I even had my buddy, the senior pastor, come up to testify about my employment and my demeanor with the children at the church. His attorney asked the question. "So is it okay for the mother to describe the father as a 'drunk'?" My pastor had the quickest and best answer, "If the shoe fits." I was disappointed that my attorney didn't go into the logistics of the evening that we had to camp out at his house during Christmas. I had been arguing for such a long time at this point that even my sister had said, "Maybe you should go to law school."

I considered it for a brief moment, but being an artist is way more fun.

My attorney and I did take some time to make amends to the court for the brief time that I had tried to represent myself. I guess that was accepted, still don't know. I also had my friend who is a florist and who had helped me to paint my Gypsy camper come up to testify that day. I was so grateful that the room was filled with folks who carried me, lifted me up, surrounded me and my children for almost eight years. It was weird really that none of my family could show up or would, as far as I knew, because it had been such a long time.

My father did ask, of course, if he needed to be present. I let him know that he probably didn't. My sister wasn't asked because she had been listening to my ex for such a long time that even she was beginning to believe his lies about me. My sister had decided that I needed additional medicine because of what had occurred to me over thirty years prior. My attorney said that she really wasn't a solid witness with that kind of crap.

Looking back on it today, I wish that we had moved forward with a drug test to include more evidence for the court. We did discuss having a nail-bed test done, which would give us up to nine months' worth of chemical information including alcohol. I wanted so bad to have that kind of money to include this but I just didn't. I didn't have the money to get my daughter a *guardian ad litem* either. The Judge said that really of course she was quite old enough to speak for herself.

His attorney tried to use some of the words to my lyrics against me that day, and of course my reply was, "It's just country music."

We all went to lunch. I had thrown everything that I had at the court including all of my monies from BMI. I had gotten a job at Panera Bread that would help me out. I also included my taxes for the last three years. Thankfully, during the final statements the Judge threw out *all* of the money issues. In fact, he was dead-on when he said, "I don't believe that this is about money anymore." Before he left the courtroom, he did something that was hilariously funny, he quoted my last song from my video *Vavavoom*. He said, "I don't believe the father looks like a home-schooling kind of guy!" I was briefly stopped by a Wilson County Sheriff storming out of the family court room that day, but I wasn't arrested. That was and is progress for me today.

So once again my ex got away with everything that he wanted. He moved to Florida.

Me and my oldest were pretty much screaming in absolute and total pain that day in court. I was furious. I stomped out afterwards and got reprimanded, but at least this time I wasn't incarcerated.

I called my sister; she thankfully had another solution. Her publisher owned a home just a few minutes away from where my ex had moved, and at least we would be able to celebrate my baby girl's thirteenth birthday there. Even that turned into another conflict with my ex, and my attorney had to step in to save her birthday party. Just recently my youngest said the best thing that my tired ears could have ever heard: "Mom, I'm ready to go back to court, and tell the judge that I will just live with you and visit them in Florida." I've been waiting over eight years for my baby to come home and perhaps this summer of 2017 she will finally have her wish and mine.

I also ripped into both the ex and the new wife when I heard about the manipulation tactics that they had tried on my daughter. I told them both, "My oldest was three years old before I had ever met this guy and his whole fucking family. I was a single mom then. I didn't need him then, and I sure as hell don't need him now."

I made sure to get the first trip that I could financially afford, and I got in my car, and I headed straight to the school where my baby had been enrolled. I got a ton of messages from the new wife about not coming down. I went down there, and to my surprise, the ex wasn't even working in Florida. The whole thing had been yet another scam.

The amount of lies continued to unfold all on their own. I guess you really do reap what you sow. I sow honesty, integrity, truth, courage in the face of every obstacle. My attorney had to continue to stay on board with every single visit. I still have no clue why the guy continues working for me when I have all but run out of money.

I found a renewed amount of energy to make it my responsibility to be present for her, and every month somehow I did it. I'm still doing it. I spoke with the women at the school in charge of my baby girl, and I made certain that they were aware of the amount of instability my baby had been through. I set up her first therapy appointment for her and will begin rebuilding our relationship in the summer of 2017.

I remember the first time my baby saw what color my eyes were; it was just during one of my visits with her in Florida in 2016. She said "Mama, your eyes are hazel!" It was a beautiful moment for me when my baby girl finally had the time and space together with me to see me clearly and without some angry person close by. Today I have more faith that my little girls will know every single detail they need to know about their Mama and that this true story will be able to give other women hope.

When my baby girl was born, she came via a c-section, and it took a few hours of time for the doctor to clear up all of the scars inside of me. That doctor said that he had never seen anything like it. He said that it looked like guitar strings, and he also said that I would never be able to have another baby because of it. I lost a ton of blood because of the amount of time that it took for my youngest to come into this world. I remember my body shivering closer to death because of it that day in the hospital. The nurses had to throw a ton of hot towels over my body to try to increase my body temperature. I'm not a nurse, but I do know a little bit about my body. I know a lot about my little girls, and I know today why I have a unique connection with my children. I may not have as much Cherokee blood as my grandmother, but I guarantee y'all that I have just enough. My bloodline is tough, and my God is the power of the whole entire universe. My God had enough power to bring my ragged ass from a homeless shelter in Lebanon, Tennessee. He certainly has more than enough power to bring my baby home. I'm still waiting for that miracle to happen.

Today I'm sitting overlooking the Old Hickory Lake where it is peaceful and hopeful. When my professors at Belmont suggested that I dig down deep and begin writing like my life depended on it, I took them seriously. I was just at Belmont the other day and got sad news that my professor David Maddox's health isn't well and it's serious enough for him to not be able to teach anymore. What my hope is today is that I am able to bring this manuscript to him before his health is too bad for him. David gave me hope, made me believe in his teachings. David always started every class with the excerpt from the Bible that day.

Today my daughter is getting on an airplane, and she is flying back home for spring break, and she just texted me to say that she "LITERALLY CAN'T WAIT!!" I am planning to make sure that she has a passport for the summer tour that I have just learned that I may be involved with because of my story online. The tour is to one hundred different cities throughout the United States and twenty different countries, so we need to apply for our passports. I have never been overseas, but I have been told by many, many different people that if I went there, I would probably never come home. My adventures continue, and they appear to get bigger and better every year. I still have my banjo man, Charles Lackey, along for the adventure, and our playing together over these last eight years has become just about flawless together. He has kept me listening to the book called "The Secret." To fill my mind with only the purest most positive thoughts. To visualize myself in my own home, with my children in my home. I have an editor, Nadia Bruce-Rawlings who has her own published books, and she lives just around the corner from me. Her book "Scars" is also a wildly amazing story about exactly how she overcame her own demons of crack cocaine.

Today I have a God box that my sister gave me in 2009, which is where I have put all of my troubles, on little tiny sheets of paper. I am trying my very best to just leave them there. It's not easy when my heart has been shredded so many different times and so many different levels. I have to continue to move forward for my kids and to keep moving forward with whatever God has planned. Today I am surrounded by people who love me and who are just beautiful smart people. I have a huge network of friends that are cheering me on towards my dreams of being the very best I can be. I have learned that if you have a problem with me, you need to speak with my "maker." My "maker" is God.

The darkest coal mines create pressure that can create diamonds after a period of time. I have decided to just be what I am, a diamond in the rough, with a little more pressure than most folks.

Song Credits

Angel in Disguise
Cecilia Diana and Lois Berg

Crazy Angel
Cecilia Diana and Lois Berg

Sudie Mae
Lois Berg

Well Behaved Cowgirls.
Lois Berg

Forever Together
Randy Finchum and Lois Berg

Play Me.
Lindsey Young and Lois Berg

Mrs. Bojangles
Jerry Jeff Walker

Running
Lois Berg

Grace & Gravity
Lois Berg

I've Seen Too Much to Give Up Now
Matraca Berg

Mama
Lois Berg

Crooked Lines
Lois Berg

Ripped
Maria Catherine Callahan and Lois Berg

Made in the USA
Lexington, KY
03 September 2017